DID YOU KNOW? SPORTS

20 THINGS YOU DIDN'T KNOW ABOUT

BASEBALL

THEIA LAKE

PowerKiDS press

Published in 2026 by The Rosen Publishing Group, Inc.
2544 Clinton Street, Buffalo, NY 14224

Copyright © 2026 by The Rosen Publishing Group, Inc.

All rights reserved. No part of this book may be reproduced in any form without permission in writing from the publisher, except by a reviewer.

Portions of this work were originally authored by Ryan Nagelhout and published as *20 Fun Facts About Baseball*. All new material in this edition was authored by Theia Lake.

Editor: Greg Roza
Book Design: Tanya Dellaccio Keeney

Photo Credits: Cover Lopolo/Shutterstock.com; p. 5 Rob Marmion/Shutterstock.com; p. 6 UrbanImages/Alamy Images; p. 7 https://upload.wikimedia.org/wikipedia/commons/a/a4/The_Pride_of_the_Yankees2.jpg; p. 8 Steve Cukrov/Shutterstock.com; p. 9 https://upload.wikimedia.org/wikipedia/commons/3/37/Union_Prisoners_at_Salisbury%2C_NC.jpg; p. 11 (top) https://upload.wikimedia.org/wikipedia/commons/5/5d/WorldSeries1903-640.jpg; p. 11 (bottom) CryptoFX/Shutterstock.com; p. 12 (A-Rod) Debby Wong/Shutterstock.com; p. 12 (Varitek) https://upload.wikimedia.org/wikipedia/commons/9/94/Jason_Varitek_on_June_30%2C_2009.jpg; p. 13 quiggyt4/Shutterstock.com; p. 14 Rob Marmion/Shutterstock.com; p. 15 Courtesy of Dave Hogg/Flickr.com; p. 16 Michael J Magee/Shutterstock.com; p. 17 Frank Romeo/Shutterstock.com; pp. 18, 21 Courtesy of the Library of Congress; p. 19 https://upload.wikimedia.org/wikipedia/commons/3/37/Lizzie_Murphy.jpg; p. 20 https://upload.wikimedia.org/wikipedia/commons/c/c3/1924_Negro_League_World_Series.jpg; p. 22 aceshot1/Shutterstock.com; p. 23 Alan C. Heison/Shutterstock.com; p. 24 https://upload.wikimedia.org/wikipedia/commons/f/f3/Nolan_Ryan_Tiger_Stadium_1990_CROP.jpg; p. 25 https://upload.wikimedia.org/wikipedia/commons/2/20/Jim_Abbott_Cannons.jpg; p. 27 https://upload.wikimedia.org/wikipedia/commons/8/88/Wambsganss%2C_and_his_tripple_%28sic%29_play_victims%2C_Kilduff%2C_Mitchell_%26_Miller_of_the_Brooklyn_B.B._Club_LCCN89712599.jpg; p. 29 meolia/Shutterstock.com.

Some of the images in this book illustrate individuals who are models. The depictions do not imply actual situations or events.

Cataloging-in-Publication Data

Names: Lake, Theia.
Title: 20 things you didn't know about baseball / Theia Lake.
Description: Buffalo, New York : PowerKids Press, 2026. | Series: Did you know? Sports | Includes glossary and index.
Identifiers: ISBN 9781499450293 (pbk.) | ISBN 9781499450309 (library bound) | ISBN 9781499450316 (ebook)
Subjects: LCSH: Baseball-Juvenile literature.
Classification: LCC GV867.5 L35 2026 | DDC 796.357-dc23

Manufactured in the United States of America

CPSIA Compliance Information: Batch #CSPK26. For Further Information contact Rosen Publishing at 1-800-237-9932.

Find us on

CONTENTS

AMERICA'S PASTIME 4
BASEBALL IN POP CULTURE. 6
BASEBALL'S BEGINNINGS 8
THE BASEBALL WAR 10
A RED-HOT RIVALRY 12
STICKY HANDS! 14
BALLPARKS 16
WOMEN IN BASEBALL 18
BASEBALL AND CIVIL RIGHTS 20
SUPER SLUGGERS 22
TOP PITCHERS 24
RARE PLAYS 26
A WEIRD, WONDERFUL GAME 28
GLOSSARY 30
FOR MORE INFORMATION 31
INDEX 32

AMERICA'S PASTIME

Baseball has long been called America's pastime. It's more than just a game. It's part of who we are as a country. Baseball has been popular in the United States since the 1800s. Great players such as Willie Mays, Babe Ruth, and Ted Williams continue to be American **legends**, long past their lifetimes.

What makes baseball such a special part of U.S. history and life? Is it the simple joys of the crack of the bat or the smell of hotdogs? Or is it something more?

BASEBALL IN POP CULTURE

DID YOU KNOW?

"Take Me Out to the Ballgame" is baseball's greatest hit!

Albert Von Tilzer and Jack Norworth wrote the song "Take Me Out to the Ballgame" in 1908. After "Happy Birthday" and the national anthem, it's the third most popular song in the United States!

Fans at Wrigley Field traditionally sing "Take Me Out to the Ballgame" during the game's seventh **inning**.

DID YOU KNOW?
Some baseball stars were also movie stars!

Babe Ruth (right) played himself in the 1942 movie *The Pride of the Yankees*, a film about player Lou Gehrig.

There are lots of famous American movies about baseball. Some even had real baseball players in them! John "Mugsy" McGraw was a Major League Baseball (MLB) player who starred in a 1915 movie called *Right Off the Bat*.

BASEBALL'S BEGINNINGS

DID YOU KNOW?
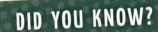
Abner Doubleday did NOT invent baseball.

Abner Doubleday was a Civil War hero. In 1907, a former pitcher named Al Spalding claimed that Doubleday invented baseball in Cooperstown, New York, in 1839. The National Baseball Hall of Fame was built in Cooperstown based on this claim. But it wasn't true!

Doubleday Field in Cooperstown, New York, is named after Abner Doubleday.

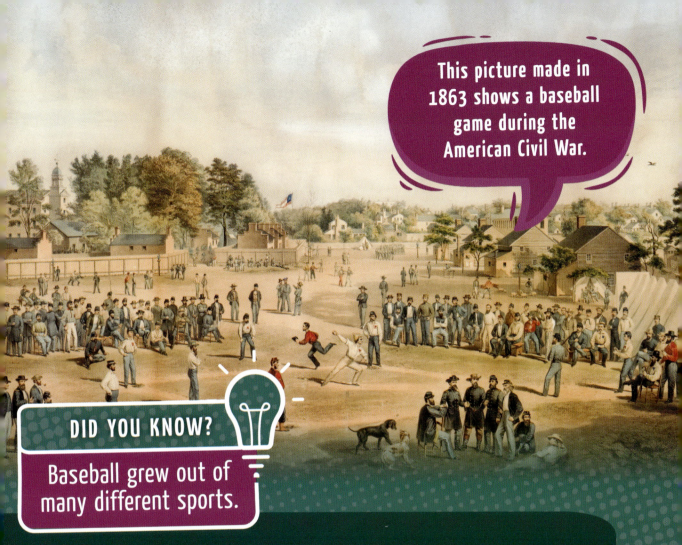

This picture made in 1863 shows a baseball game during the American Civil War.

DID YOU KNOW?
Baseball grew out of many different sports.

Baseball may be based on the English games of cricket and rounders. During the 1800s, a group called the Knickerbocker Base Ball Club of New York invented many of the rules that would shape baseball.

THE BASEBALL WAR

DID YOU KNOW?

The National League (NL) and the American League (AL) were **rivals** until they came together to form Major League Baseball in 1903.

The NL is the oldest U.S. major league baseball group that's still in play. It started in 1876. The AL was formed later, around 1901.

In 1903, the two rival leagues came to an agreement that stated both the AL and NL were major leagues. The winners of the two leagues would play in a World Series each year. The first World Series was played between the Boston Americans and Pittsburgh Pirates in 1903.

1903 WORLD SERIES

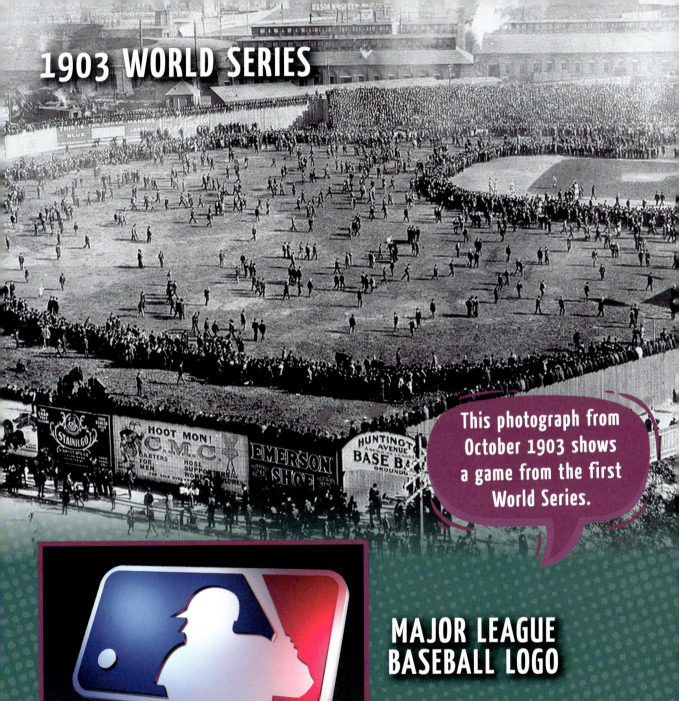

This photograph from October 1903 shows a game from the first World Series.

MAJOR LEAGUE BASEBALL LOGO

A RED-HOT RIVALRY

DID YOU KNOW?
The Yankees and the Red Sox have a famous, **fierce** rivalry.

The New York Yankees and the Boston Red Sox are both part of the AL. That means they've never played a World Series game against each other. But they have faced off in other games, which were marked by their fierceness.

A-ROD

JASON VARITEK

Yankees batter Alex Rodriguez (nicknamed "A-Rod") and Red Sox catcher Jason Varitek famously got into a fight during a 2004 game.

DID YOU KNOW?

The Yankees-Red Sox rivalry started with the curse of the "Bambino"!

The Red Sox swept the Cardinals in the 2004 World Series.

The "Bambino" was one of Babe Ruth's nicknames. When Ruth was sold from the Red Sox to the Yankees in 1919, the Yankees did very well. The Red Sox didn't play in another World Series until 2004, over 80 years later!

STICKY HANDS!

DID YOU KNOW?

All MLB baseballs are rubbed with special mud!

New baseballs are hard to grip, or hold tightly. Rubbing them with mud helps! The mud, called Lena Blackburne Baseball Rubbing Mud, has been used for decades in the majors. It comes from the banks of the Delaware River.

The MLB has rules about how to put mud on baseballs properly.

> This is the baseball bat used by George Brett in what came to be called "the pine tar incident."

DID YOU KNOW?

Bat handles can be covered with pine tar to make them easier to grip.

There are rules about pine tar use. Only the first 18 inches (46 cm) of a bat handle can be covered with it. In 1983, Kansas City **slugger** George Brett was called out after hitting a home run against the Yankees. The umpires said there was too much pine tar on his bat!

BALLPARKS

DID YOU KNOW?
Fenway Park is the oldest Major League ballpark.

The first game in Fenway Park was played on April 20, 1912. This park has some quirks, or oddities, including a 37-foot- (11.3 m) high wall called the Green Monster. Pesky's Pole is the right field foul pole and is just 302 feet (92 m) from home plate.

Eleven World Series have been played at Fenway Park.

DID YOU KNOW?

The Home Run Apple pops up whenever the Mets hit a home run!

When the Mets moved to Citi Field in 2009, a new Home Run Apple was made. The old apple now stands outside Citi Field.

In 1980, Shea Stadium made a change to draw in crowds. They built a huge apple inside a hat! The Home Run Apple would pop out of a hat whenever the Mets hit a home run.

WOMEN IN BASEBALL

DID YOU KNOW?

Women have been playing baseball since the 1860s.

The Vassar Resolutes was the first organized team of women players. They wore ankle-length wool dresses when they played! Sadly, the Resolutes were forced to disband, or stop playing, in 1878.

This photograph of a female baseball player was taken in 1913.

To this day, Lizzie Murphy is still the only woman to have ever played with a team of major leaguers in a big-league ballpark.

DID YOU KNOW?

"The Queen of Baseball" was the first person to play on both AL and NL All-Star Teams.

Lizzie Murphy was the first woman to play **professional** baseball. Murphy played a few innings at first base with the American League All-Stars in 1922 in a game against the Boston Red Sox. In 1928, she played in an All-Star Game with the National League All-Stars.

BASEBALL AND CIVIL RIGHTS

DID YOU KNOW?

During the 1920s, 30s, and 40s, Black players played on Negro Leagues.

Segregation was the forced separation of the races. Because of segregation, Black baseball players were barred from many major and minor leagues. In 1920, "Rube" Foster formed the Negro National League. Other Negro leagues formed later.

This picture was taken at the 1924 Colored World Series when the Negro National League champions faced off against the Eastern Colored League champions.

Robinson's entry to the MLB marked the beginning of desegregation in baseball. Baseball was desegregated before the military (armed forces) was.

DID YOU KNOW?

Jackie Robinson was the first Black Major League Baseball player.

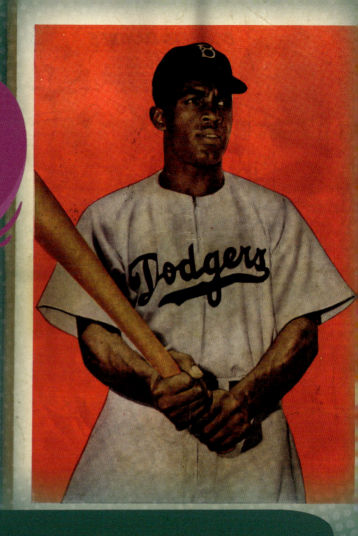

Jackie Robinson was signed by the Brooklyn Dodgers in 1946, making him the first Black MLB player. Robinson was a baseball star! He was also a leader in the Civil Rights Movement, standing beside Martin Luther King Jr. in the fight for equal rights.

SUPER SLUGGERS

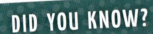

DID YOU KNOW?

Pete Rose holds the record for the most hits in Major League Baseball.

Nicknamed "Charlie Hustle," Pete Rose had 4,256 hits during his 24 years playing baseball. He reached this record in 1985, beating the last record holder, Ty Cobb, who had 4,189 hits. Although he was a record-breaking hitter, Rose was banned from baseball in 1989 because of betting crimes.

This statue of Pete Rose is outside the American Ballpark in Cincinnati, Ohio.

Suzuki had 242 hits in 2001, his rookie—or first—season!

DID YOU KNOW?

Ichiro Suzuki holds the record for most hits in a season.

In 2004, Ichiro Suzuki, nicknamed "The Wizard," broke an 84-year hitting record. Previously, George Sisler had held the record, with 257 hits in a season. Suzuki finished with 262 hits. That was 101 more hits than he played games that year.

TOP PITCHERS

DID YOU KNOW?
Nolan Ryan holds the record for most strikeouts—5,714!

During his 27-year career, Ryan pitched for the New York Mets, California Angels, Houston Astros, and Texas Rangers. Ryan has more "Ks"—5,714—than innings pitched—5,386. Ryan leads all other pitchers by more than 800 strikeouts. Ryan also holds Major League records with 2,795 walks and seven career no-hitters.

No-hitters are complete games without allowing a hit.

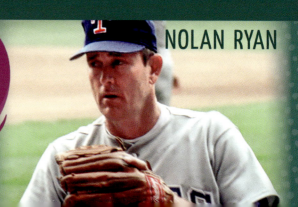

NOLAN RYAN

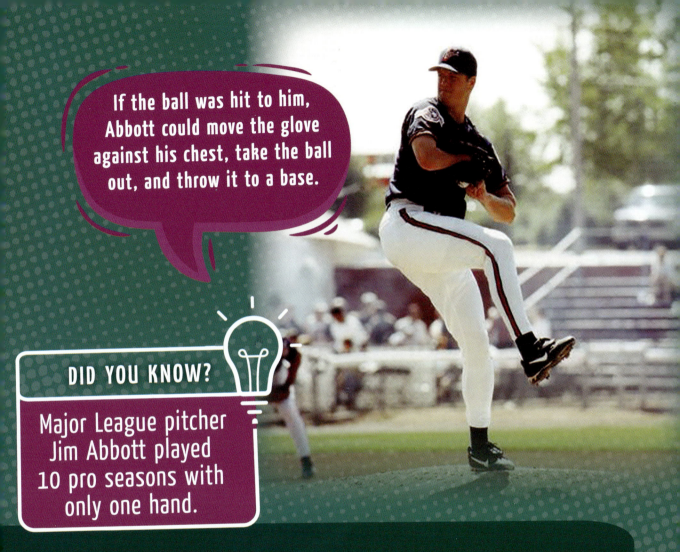

> If the ball was hit to him, Abbott could move the glove against his chest, take the ball out, and throw it to a base.

DID YOU KNOW?

Major League pitcher Jim Abbott played 10 pro seasons with only one hand.

Jim Abbott was born without a right hand. From a young age he loved baseball and was a skillful player. He would pitch, then put a glove on his throwing hand. While pitching for the Yankees, Abbott threw a no-hitter against Cleveland.

RARE PLAYS

DID YOU KNOW?
Some plays are so rare, or uncommon, they've happened only once in MLB history!

An unassisted triple play is when a player gets all three outs in an inning without help from other fielders. There have been only 15 unassisted triple plays in the history of Major League Baseball.

Only once has a team had two unassisted triple plays in a single game! The Minnesota Twins turned two triple plays during a game against the Boston Red Sox in July 1990. In spite of this rare feat, the Red Sox still won the game!

BASEBALL STATS

BA
BATTING AVERAGE
The number of hits a player has divided by his number of bats.

E
ERROR
A mistake made by a player in the field.

RBI
RUNS BATTED IN
The number of runners brought home by a player when at the plate.

R
RUN
A point given to a team when a player reaches home safely.

ERA
EARNED RUN AVERAGE
The number of earned runs a pitcher allows divided by how many innings he pitched, multiplied by nine.

H
HIT
A ball put in play that lets a batter reach base safely.

SO (K)
STRIKEOUT
When a pitcher throws three strikes or a batter swings and misses three times.

OBP
ON BASE PERCENTAGE
The number of times a batter reaches base divided by his plate appearances.

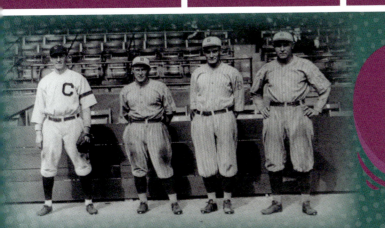

In 1920, Cleveland second baseman Bill Wambsganss (left) made an unassisted triple play in the World Series.

A WEIRD, WONDERFUL GAME!

Baseball is a weird and wonderful game full of fun facts. Did you know the longest baseball game in Major League history went 25 innings? They had to stop the game and finish it another day! Then there's this wild fact: Reds catching great Johnny Bench could hold seven baseballs in his bare hand.

The stats, records, and amazing players are part of what makes baseball so fun to watch—and play! What might the **future** hold for this all-American game?

GLOSSARY

champion: The winner of first place in a competition.

fierce: Strong or aggressive.

future: Time to come.

inning: A division of time in a baseball game during which both teams get a chance at bat. A professional game has 9 innings.

legend: A person about whom exciting stories are told.

professional: Having to do with something a person does for money.

rivals: One of two groups competing against each other.

slugger: In baseball, a powerful batter.

traditionally: In a way that's traditional, or having to do with the ways of doing things in a culture that are passed down from parents to children.

FOR MORE INFORMATION

BOOKS

James, India. *Baseball*. St. Catharine's, Ontario: Crabtree Publishing, 2024.

Troupe, Thomas Kingsley. *Baseball*. Minnetonka, MN: Kaleidoscope Publishing, 2023.

WEBSITES

Major League Baseball

www.mlb.com

Check out stats, games, and more on the MLB site.

National Baseball Hall of Fame

www.baseballhall.org

Learn more about the greatest players of all time!

Publisher's note to educators and parents: Our editors have carefully reviewed these websites to ensure that they are suitable for students. Many websites change frequently, however, and we cannot guarantee that a site's future contents will continue to meet our high standards of quality and educational value. Be advised that students should be closely supervised whenever they access the internet.

INDEX

A

American League (AL), 10, 12, 19

D

Doubleday, Abner, 8

H

home run, 15, 17

L

Lana Blackburne Baseball Rubbing Mud, 14

M

Major League Baseball (MLB), 7, 10, 14, 21, 22, 24, 25, 26, 28

N

National Baseball Hall of Fame, 8

National League (NL), 10, 19

Negro leagues, 20

T

"Take Me Out to the Ballgame," 6

W

women, 18, 19

World Series, 10, 11, 12, 13, 16, 27